MW01289982

Martin R. Phillips

ANCIENT

EGYPT

Disclaimer: All attempts have been made by the author to provide factual and accurate content. No responsibility will be taken by the author or publisher for any damages caused by misuse of the content described in this book. The content of this book has been derived from various sources. A pen name may have been used to protect the privacy of the author. Please consult an expert before attempting anything described in this book.

Hill Tech Ventures Inc.
Publishing Division | Nanaimo, Canada
Printed in the United States

ANCIENT

EGYPT

Discover the Secrets of

Ancient Egypt

MARTIN R. PHILLIPS

ABOUT THE AUTHOR

MARTIN R. PHILLIPS

 Martin R. Phillips is an extremely passionate historian, archaeologist, and most recently a writer. Ever since Martin was a young boy he has been fascinated with ancient cultures and civilizations.

In 1990, Martin graduated with distinction from the University of Cambridge with a double major in History and Archaeology. Upon graduation, Martin worked as an archeologist and travelled the world working in various excavation sites. Over the years, while working as an archaeologist, Martin became very well cultured and gained great insights into some of the most historic civilizations to ever exist. This first hand insight into the ancient cultures of the world is what sparked Martin's newest passion, history writing and story telling.

In 2012, Martin decided to retire from archeology to focus on writing. Over the years he has seen and experienced a great deal of fascinating things from all over world. Martin now spends the majority of his free time putting all of his research, experience, and thoughts onto paper in an attempt to share his knowledge of the ancient cultures with the world.

Over the past few years Martin has excelled in his writings. His narrative style has a way of combining the cold hard facts with a story teller's intrigue which makes for an excellent reading experience.

"Live your life to the fullest and enjoy the journey!"

- Martin R. Phillips

TABLE OF CONTENTS

INTRODUCTION

Ancient Egypt is one of the most fascinating civilizations that the world has ever seen. From looming pyramids to intricate monoliths; from kings and pharaohs to the waters of the Nile, Egypt's history is one in which we can see the potential of humanity.

Even today, while there are some theories, we are not certain how the ancient Egyptians built many of their monuments, including the pyramids. The civilization of Egypt was home to some of the most profound thought of the time, some of the most incredible inventions and some of the most famous rulers throughout history.

So what is it about Ancient Egypt that has fascinated us for millennia and continues to pique our interest today?

There seems to be a unique spirit to the ancient Egyptians. The Egyptian way of life seems to be almost anachronistic in a lot of ways. They had primitive batteries (we still don't know why,) they were fans of board games, women enjoyed more freedom in ancient Egypt than they did in other civilizations, in many cases for thousands of years to come, they had house pets, used a form of chewing gum made from myrrh and wax and some Egyptian doctors actually specialized in different areas of medicine.

Providing exact dates to events in ancient Egypt can be quite difficult, and in some cases impossible, as the ancient Egyptians did not use a standardized system of chronology as we do today. The ancient Egyptians would instead use the length of their pharaohs' reigns as a way of telling the year. While this may have been useful enough at the time, it's difficult for researchers nowadays to pinpoint at exactly which time the fourth year of Khufu was. In most cases we don't know exactly when these pharaohs reigned, or even how close we are to a complete list of pharaohs. Therefore, dates in this book will focus more on a dynastic timeline with modern calendar years being added in where possible.

The history, culture and symbolism of ancient Egypt is still popular today, over two thousand years later. There are many things to be fascinated about in regard to ancient Egypt. But what made them who they were? What drove them to settle where they settled, live how they lived and create such an enigmatic and captivating civilization? How were the Egyptians able to sustain their civilization for nearly three thousand years?

These and many other questions will be covered in these pages. I invite you to sit back, relax and enjoy learning about what is quite possibly the most important and interesting ancient civilizations the world has ever seen.

Thanks again, I hope you enjoy it!

CHAPTER 1

Agriculture and Moving Toward Dynasty

The history of ancient Egyptian civilization (or Kemet – The Black Land as it was known during the Old Kingdom) begins and ends with the Nile River, referred to in ancient Egypt as Iteru, or Great River. It is the largest river in the world in regard to length. (The Amazon drains more water, but the Nile is longer.) The Nile is not only notable for its length, but its regularity, its navigability and its smooth currents. This is such an important thing to Egypt (ancient and present) because of its use in agriculture.

Egypt for the most part is a desert, but with the fertile water of the Nile which floods every year, people were able to set up settlements and a whole civilization around its shores. The silt and mineral deposits left by the flooding of the Nile literally made the ground so fertile that ancient Egyptians would cast their seeds over the soft earth and let their livestock walk over it, thereby "planting" their crops.

The civilizations of Egypt were primarily right along the banks of the river. The navigability of the river allowed the inhabitants to send resources along its currents for trade, and the fertile land made crop-growing easy enough that people had more time to focus on different aspects of their lives.

The Nile wasn't without its perils however. Along with alligators and crocodiles, the yearly flooding was often unpredictable in size. Some years this led to increased flooding which would deluge towns and cities along the Nile River Valley. At others, the flood would not be high enough; crops would suffer and people would starve.

Prior to wide-spread settling along the Nile River Valley, the peoples of Egypt were largely nomadic. They would hunt large prey in the fertile lands of the Sahara (this is before it became the world's biggest desert.) This all changed with the climate shift of approximately 5,000 B.C. The land dried up and larger animals were unable to continue to live in the area. The Nile quickly became the only source of water in the area.

Before Egypt was united, it consisted of Upper Egypt and Lower Egypt. Upper Egypt is called as such due to its location nearer the source of the Nile River. The rulers of Upper Egypt wore a long, white crown. This crown was known as the Hedjet. It symbolized power and divine right to the subjects of Upper Egypt.

Lower Egypt began at the Mediterranean Sea in the north and ran upstream on the Nile to the south, meeting its end at the boundary of Upper Egypt with a cataract, or river rapid near Aswan. The kings of Lower Egypt wore a red crown called the Deshret. It too represented a divine right, and one or both crowns were often depicted on the god Horus, who was believed to be the ruler from whom the kings and pharaohs inherited the throne.

Why so much focus on the crowns of Upper and Lower Egypt? It was the unification of these crowns that would signify a unified Egypt. This begins with a man named Narmer. Narmer was king of Upper-Egypt. Historians are unsure if other rulers of the time were actually this man, or if Narmer was a representative of multiple kingships during the unification of Upper and Lower Egypt.

Most of what we know about Narmer can be traced back to the Narmer Palette. The Narmer Palette depicts Narmer with both crowns of Egypt and hitting an enemy with a flail or mace. It is the earliest depiction of a king wearing both crowns and thus suggests that the battle depicted in the palette was the final battle that granted him the kingship over both Upper and Lower Egypt.

As the story goes, however, Narmer (possibly Menes, Aha or Scorpion) unified the previously rival lands of

Upper and Lower Egypt in 3150 B.C. He did this through administrative and militaristic means. He was the first king to wear the double-crown, the crowns of Upper and Lower Egypt, the Hedjet and the Deshret. This symbolized the union of Egypt into one nation, ruled by a single man and unified through culture and political means.

Along with unifying Egypt, he also founded the city of Memphis – "Balance of Two Lands" (also called Inbu-Hedj meaning "white walls") which would serve as Egypt's capitol for many dynasties. A dynasty is a string of rulers, generally of the same bloodline. The city was surrounded on all sides by large walls. This protected the city from the flooding of the Nile while allowing it to be in the prime location for farming, trade and travel.

Narmer is said to have ruled for a period of about sixty years. During this time, Egypt became ever more united, religion and spirituality were promulgated and the land flourished. The death of Narmer is disputed today, but original records say that he was killed by a hippopotamus.

Along with the unification of Upper Egypt to the south and Lower Egypt to the north, the civilizations on the east and west sides of the river Nile would come to be unified. This was important to the Egyptians for religious reasons, due to their belief that in the East, where the sun rises, was symbolized new life, growth and prosperity, whereas the west, the direction of the setting sun, symbolized death and the afterlife. This can be noted throughout the civilization of the time as many burial grounds were located on the western banks of the Nile and the east contained most settlements and temples.

The rule of Narmer is commonly referred to as the dynasty 0.

Dynasties 1 and 2 comprise the time period most commonly known as the early dynastic period or the archaic period. It is during this time period that the earliest examples Egyptian writing can be found. This period is marked by the transition from a pre-dynastic Egypt to a civilization more familiar to us as Ancient Egypt. The archaic period lasted from around 3100-2686 BC.

CHAPTER 2

The Old Kingdom

Just like societies today, the social structure of the old kingdom was mostly made up of skilled and unskilled laborers, craftsmen, farmers, etc. This group made up the largest population by far, but these people enjoyed fewer rights and privileges than all of the other classes. Above them were the richer nobles and local leaders who enjoyed a level of affluence which escaped all but the luckiest of the working class members. Directly above the nobles in power were the priests, and above them sat the pharaoh.

It wasn't until the third dynasty that The Old Kingdom began. The old kingdom existed between 2686 and 2333 BC, and was a crucial period for the Egyptians. The old kingdom lasted between the third and sixth dynasties. It's during the old kingdom that we find some of the most iconic structures that the world has ever known: the pyramids.

It was in the third dynasty that King Djoser commissioned the first pyramid to be built. It was to be a burial tomb, and was created out of stone. This step-pyramid is located at Saqqara, and can still be seen today.

Although it wasn't until the fifth dynasty that texts would be set down to later be discovered by archaeologists regarding the funerary beliefs of the Ancient Egyptians, it's likely that these traditions went back a ways further, possibly to pre-dynastic Egypt.

Ancient Egyptians believed that a body must be preserved in order to reach the afterlife intact, and that even having an afterlife was decided by the gods, most notably, the pharaoh.

Viewed as not only a king, but the intermediary between the gods and man, the pharaoh wielded a great deal of power and demanded great respect, not only from the common people, but nobles as well. In order to reach the afterlife, it was considered necessary that an individual must have a purpose there. The pharaoh was a shoo-in, due to the fact of his leadership and pre-selection as a god among men. Along with the pharaoh, human sacrifices were common, usually so the pharaoh would have servants in the afterlife. Pretty bleak, huh? Along with this, it was necessary for a person to prove his or her worth in life so that they could be considered worthy of taking part in the afterlife.

One of the most predominant concepts of ancient belief was Ma'at: living a truthful, balanced, lawful, moral and just life. Ma'at was also a goddess in Ancient Egypt whose feather would be the counterweight placed against the weight of a person's heart. Those who lived just lives (those whose hearts weighed equal or less than that of Ma'at's feather) would enjoy an afterlife in paradise, or Aaru. Those whose hearts outweighed the feather would be doomed to live in the underworld (Duat) for eternity and the heart would be eaten by Ammit, the soul eater. That's why it's a good idea to live a light-hearted life. (The author would like to apologize here; however, it should be noted that no history book is complete without at least one bad pun. Let's all hope that's the only one.)

As the in-depth mythological beliefs of the ancient Egyptians are investigated at length in another volume of this series, it is outside of the scope of this present work to delve too deeply into Egyptian mythology where it doesn't specifically concern the history of the Ancient Egyptians.

In earlier periods in Egypt, the dead were simply buried in the arid ground. This would preserve them due to a lack of moisture. Over time, those with a greater amount of affluence would be buried in small tombs called mastabas.

It was in these mastabas that the pharaohs before Djoser were buried. The issue with mastabas, however, was that the bodies would rot in a way that they hadn't in the arid ground, due to the cooler temperatures which caused a greater amount of moisture to collect inside them. This sent the Egyptians on the path toward a different kind of body-preservation, and one that comes quick to mind at the mere mention of ancient Egypt.

Mummification is the process of preserving the bodies through removal of the organs (although this was a later addition to the process,) use of embalming fluid and wrapping of the body in long strips of cloth. When embalmers did start to remove the organs (sometime around the fourth dynasty,) all of the organs (with the notable exception of the heart for reasons seen above) were removed in order to preserve it for the afterlife.

Not only were bodies that were considered worthy of a shot at the afterlife preserved, possessions of the dead were also buried with them. Depending on a person's wealth, these possessions would include coins, jewels, pots and other luxuries but also sometimes included servants and pets. It was believed that what a person was buried or entombed with would go with them into the afterlife.

For kings, pharaohs and richer nobles, mummifica tion was a privilege, however, most commoners likely continued to be buried in the sand.

It was during the time of Djoser, however, that the first pyramid was built. Djoser's architect Imhotep (also a physician, engineer, chancellor to Djoser, a carpenter, sculptor and high-priest... imagine that paycheck) is credited with designing the first pyramid in Egypt, the above-mentioned Pyramid of Djoser at Saqqara. This would be the first, but far from the last or greatest pyramid constructed throughout Egypt.

It was during the fourth dynasty that some of the most recognizable pyramids were built. The first of the fourth dynasty's pharaohs, Sneferu is thought to have ordered the construction of up to three pyramids. It was his son Khufu, however, that would be responsible for ordering and overseeing construction of the great pyramid of Giza.

Although it is commonly thought that the pyramids were built by an enormous population of slaves, evidence suggests that this work was actually bought and paid for. Not much is known about the specific methods involved, though many theories do exist (including, but not limited to aliens.) What the evidence does show, however, is that the pyramids were built by peasants who were fed, housed and paid while their fields were submerged during the annual flooding of the Nile.

During the time of the old kingdom, previously autonomous and independent portions of Egypt fell under the sole ruler of the pharaoh. This led to some perks, but also placed a much greater deal of responsibility on the pharaoh as he or she would then have to assume the duties which would previously have been performed by the regional governors.

In 2495 BC began the fifth dynasty. This would be a dynasty where pyramids were still constructed to a point, but they were not nearly on such a grand scale as those of Sneferu and Khufu. This period did not see cessation of all impressive buildings, however. During the fifth dynasty, temples to Ra, the sun god and chief deity of Egypt were constructed and cults of Ra became more and more prominent.

The period of the fifth dynasty saw a large increase in trade with merchants travelling not only along the Nile, but over the Mediterranean Sea as well. This was one of the important changes during the fifth dynasty that likely affected the future of the old kingdom.

By the sixth dynasty, the nobles of Egypt began to grow richer; in some cases, even moreso than the king. It is theorized that this actually happened due to the pharaoh's levying a lighter tax burden on the wealthier and more favored individuals of the kingdom. This process led to super-wealthy nobility, and an increasingly pocket-poor state. Evidence of this can be witnessed in the grandiose tombs of the nobility and the lesser tombs of the pharaohs during this period.

Between the increase in trade and regional affluence, the power of the pharaohs diminished in favor of local leaders known as nomarchs. Nomarchs were rulers of their respective regions, and power was actually given to them, in most cases, by the pharaoh himself in order to make wider rule of all of Egypt more efficient. As time went on, however, these nomarchs formed their own dynasties independent of the pharaoh bloodline and thus led to a tumultuous sixth dynasty.

Things came to a head when Pepi II was pharaoh. He lived and ruled an unusually long time. This caused many issues, including Pepi II outliving his heirs. The bloodline of the pharaohs was lost, and within a short amount of time, unrest and disorder swept through the land. The nail in the coffin where the sixth dynasty and the old kingdom itself finally came effectively to an end was a period of lower flood-levels from the Nile. This left the crops sparse, the people hungry and the temperament of the people irritable to say the very least.

It wasn't until this all-encompassing power of the pharaoh started to languish that the old kingdom came to an end.

CHAPTER **3**

Collapse and Rebirth

The time of the first intermediate period was a time marred by conflict in Egypt. The power of the pharaohs had become weakened to the point that they were often ineffective against the regional leaders, the nomarchs. The nomarchs wielded power over the forty-two major cities, or nomes, and as the power of the pharaohs became ever more diminished, these rulers stepped in the fill the gaps.

The first intermediate period was likely not due to a shift in power, but a shift in water. The flooding of the Nile, such a crucial yearly event, had been especially low. Crops were lost and famine was widespread.

Although the power of the pharaohs was diminished, it wasn't gone completely. The seventh through tenth dynasties were during this time, and part of the eleventh dynasty was also during this period.

Not too much is known of the seventh and eighth dynasties, however, it is generally regarded that the seventh dynasty consisted of oligarchical rule, that is, rule by a few elite individuals as opposed to a kingship. It was also written by a historian and priest Manetho that there was at one point seventy kings within seventy days, however, this is commonly dismissed as hyperbole. A couple of likely explanations of this claim are that kingship was heavily disputed and no king held pharaohship for long. Another possibility is that, due to the rise of feuding power structures within Egypt, there were more than one king at a time who either ruled a portion of the land, or claimed to be ruler of all Egypt. The truth of the matter is that although many claimed power during this period, Egypt was, for all intents and purposes, anarchic.

Unfortunately, apart from Manetho, who was from a much later period of time, during the Greek rule of Egypt, there is precious little preserved about the first intermediate period. Not only that, we do not have, at least to our present knowledge, the actual works from Manetho's hands. All that we have of his writings are from other historians who must have had some knowledge or experience with Manetho's writings, at least enough that they referenced them. The problem here is that we don't know what would have been Manetho's word, and what would have been the word of the later historians.

The eighth dynasty, like those before it, ruled from Memphis. It's often postulated that these rulers claimed heirship due to the bloodline of the sixth dynasty which they claimed to have possessed, however, not much is known about this dynasty.

The ninth dynasty was the first to rule from outside of Memphis. These rulers affected their control from Herakleopolis (a Greek name, given to this city much later, meaning "City of Hercules." It's possible that the ninth dynasty saw a reunification of Egypt; however, this did not stand for long. The first king of this dynasty was said to have been of choleric temperament and took out his aggression on the people of Egypt.

During the first intermediate period, power was more or less split between Thebes and Memphis, although the Herakleopolitan rulers did see a great increase in power during this time. Due to the schism, there are relatively distinct architecture and artistic influences depending on the region from whence they came.

One of the most important things regarding the art referring to this period lies in the "literature" around the beginning of the middle kingdom. Much of this literature was in the form of laments, or lamentations. Lamentations are cries, writings, basically some form of expression where the person lamenting is trying to express their sadness or loss of hope. As these lamentations are generally regarded as either fictional or unreliable accounts of history, it's difficult to tell where actual events stop and the imagination of the writer or scribe begins, however, from these, we can deduce some things about the first intermediate period.

One of the lamentations suggests that Egypt was invaded by foreigners. This would have been the first known instance of an invasion by a faction outside of Egypt itself (although it would be far from the last.) Whether it was a military invasion, immigration or happened at all is uncertain, but the scribe goes on to suggest that the old order of things within Egypt had more or less been dissolved. Slave girls, the writer of this lamentation would say, were decked out in gold and other precious metals and jewels. By this can be extrapolated that the old order of the king or pharaoh having the most, then the nobles having much, etc. on down the line, was upset, and the Egyptians were not a people geared toward change.

This particular lamentation also alludes to many instances of grave-robbing and class warfare, particularly in the guise of attack of the nobles and the wealthy by the commoners. Other lamentations are more focused on spiritual ideals, but all seem to describe a yearning to return to the times of glory under Sneferu, the original builder of pyramids. Whether this longing had anything to do with the rise of the middle kingdom or not is uncertain, however, all sources suggest a great deal of unrest and unhappiness during this period between 2181 and 2040 B.C.

So much grave-robbing happened during the first intermediate period, in fact, that it wasn't just the tombs of the commoners or the nobility that were robbed; targets also included the great pyramids of Giza. One can only imagine what treasures of history may have been found in Khufu's pyramid, or Sneferu's, or any one of countless other sites looted during this time. Unfortunately, however, the greed and disorder of the time led to the loss of whatever artifacts may have been found. In fact, not only were things normally considered to be valuables taken, but in a lot of cases, the sarcophagi, body included, were removed.

But that was about to change.

This isn't to say that all of the power was consolidated with the pharaoh, in fact, a great deal of the regional leadership would come from local governors. However, these governors would come to be united under the pharaoh. It wasn't an easy process at first. The pharaoh had to actually ask these governors to send men for the purpose of army-building, however, it wouldn't be long until the pharaohs yielded the kind of power that they had during the old kingdom.

The eleventh dynasty is marked by a great deal of struggle for these kings to gain this power and unification. It is with the eleventh dynasty that rule begins from the city of Thebes. One of the interesting things about both dynasties of the middle kingdom is that many of the leaders had the same name or, more accurately, their names began with the same word. In the eleventh dynasty, the name was Intef.

This has made tracing the history of this period a bit difficult at times, as papyri and tablets recovered are often degraded or fragmented. This is such a problem in that often times the full name of the pharaoh is not present, and thus it can be difficult to say with certainty from these sources, exactly which king did what. Some things are known though.

There was a progression from the first king Intef, whose full name was Intef Sehertawi (or Seher-towi, Seher-tawi, etc.) which roughly translates to "Causing Peace Between Two Lands." This is a reference to the fragmented Egypt, and although this king was far from pharaoh of all Egypt, it begins to signify an intention toward reunification and consolidation of power. Although his name inferred a bringer of peace or at least pacification, Sehertawi began waging war against the leaders of the north, which did lead to a greater amount of control to the dynastic rulers of Thebes.

After Intef Sehertawi came Intef Wahankh, or "Established in Life." Wahankh (or Wah-Ankh) consolidated the Upper Kingdom under his rule and battled with the rulers of the north for greater control of Egypt. This finally ended with Wahankh gaining control of the important city of Abydos. Apart from this, not much is known about Intef Wahankh, other than the fact that he was a great lover of his dogs. In 1860, a stelé was found of this king whose funerary stelé had five dogs on it, presumably his.

It was with Intef Nakht Neb Tep Nefer (or Nakht-nebtepnefer,) or "beautiful and mighty lord," that a much larger effort was made in order to fully reunify the Upper and Lower Kingdoms whose close ties had been severed, or at least frayed, near the end of the old kingdom into the first intermediate period. He led a military expedition from Thebes in the south, or the Upper Kingdom against the people of the north, the Lower Kingdom.

The Lower Kingdom was still under the rule of the tenth dynasty of the Herakleopolitan rulers (not to be confused with the tenth dynasty of Egypt which had since passed) and, like most rulers the world has known, they weren't very willing to give up their power without a fight, and a fight is exactly what they gave. Many battles were fought and would continue to be fought between the Theban kings of the south and the Herakleopolitan kings of the north.

CHAPTER 4

Pharaohs and the Middle Kingdom

It was during the eleventh dynasty that Egypt would finally become stable and united under one rule. It was during the reign of Mentuhotep II that the bickering and disjunct powers would become consolidated and the rule of Egypt would rest once more into the hands of the pharaoh. The middle kingdom would last from 2134 to 1782 B.C.

The middle kingdom came into being at or around the thirty-ninth year of Mentuhotep II's rule. Mentuhotep II's Horus name was Se-ankh-ib-towi, or "Making the Heart of the Two Lands Alive/To Live." There is debate as to whether Mentuhotep II was or wasn't the son of the last Intef, Intef Nakhtnebtepnefer, but it is certain that his rule would bring a great change to Egypt.

It was his mission to complete the intention of his forefathers and bring the land of Lower Egypt under his control and thus unify the country once more under a single ruler. He sent a military campaign against the Herakleopolitans during a revolt in one of the nomes to the north.

Much of what we know about Mentuhotep comes from his burial site. It was a departure from the burial sites of previous kings in many ways, although in the center did stand a small pyramid. Much of the actual structure of the mortuary temple is gone or in ruin today, however, some things survived which give us an insight into the times.

For instance there is a mass grave holding sixty or more mummified young men was discovered. These men were not children, but they were young, probably twenties to thirties, and they showed signs of being killed in battle. From this, we can extrapolate some of the violence and warfare which occurred during the battles for reunification under Mentuhotep's rule.

Along with this, we see caskets in the harem section of the complex which housed not only the mummified remains of those who died around this time, but spells and incantations to assist the dead in making their way to the land of the dead, spells intending to help these people be resurrected on the other side. At the end of the fifth dynasty, the pharaoh Unas was the first to have ritual texts in his pyramid chamber, but these beliefs were expanding to include incantations written out inside of the sarcophagus. This speaks to an even more important sense of religion during the beginning of the middle kingdom than was apparent in the old.

Mentuhotep II was the first pharaoh in quite a while to identify himself as a god among men. He wore a headdress of two gods, Min and Amun (or Amoun.) During the eleventh dynasty, Amun would become the god of Thebes, or the patron god of Thebes. Amun was the god of the wind and, during much of Egypt's history, the king of the gods.

The middle kingdom was a time of great expansion. Military outposts rose up in various parts of Egypt's spreading area of influence. As the borders of Egypt expanded, so did the power of the pharaohs. Although the middle kingdom only saw two dynasties (the eleventh and twelfth,) it was a time of great power and growth for not only the pharaohs, but for the people of Egypt as well.

When Mentuhotep II died after a reign of over fifty years, kingship passed on to his son, Mentuhotep III or Mentuhotep Se-Ankh-Ka-Re. It was with Mentuhotep III that more expeditions would be undertaken and fortresses built. These forts were often built larger than necessary for purposes of intimidation. The power of Egypt was back, and the pharaohs wanted their enemies to know it.

Although Mentuhotep III would only reign for twelve years, much can be extrapolated about the state of the pharaohs during this time. One of the most profound indications that the pharaoh's power was growing to a point that hadn't been seen since before the first intermediate period was the expedition to the Wadi Hammamat.

The goal of this expedition was to bring back fine, black stone, gum, perfume and incense. Without some context, this may sound like a simple task and a simple journey, but the expedition to the land of Wadi Hammamat was over arid deserts, over which, the 3,000 men who made the journey not only drove out marauders, but dug twelve individual wells in order to sustain the men. Along with this, it is said that each of the men would carry two jugs of water, both for his own use; and that pack animals, most likely donkeys, carried containers full of extra sandals, due to the short life of footwear under these conditions. Such an expedition hadn't been attempted since the old kingdom, and it was quite the statement of the growing power of the pharaoh.

After Mentuhotep III came Mentuhotep IV, or Neb-Towi-Re (or Nebtawire, Neb-Tawi-Re, etc.) whose name meant something to the effect of, "Re is the lord of the two lands." As if the expedition of 3,000 men by his father wasn't enough, Mentuhotep IV sent another expedition to Wadi Hammamat, only this time, he more than tripled the number of men to 10,000.

Of the last king of the eleventh dynasty, Mentuhotep IV, not much else is known. In fact, other than inscriptions in the Wadi Hammamat regarding the expedition of the 10,000 men, the histories of the time regarded the seven years when Mentuhotep would have been pharaoh as seven empty years. It is, however, likely that his vizier (an advisor, esp. to royalty) succeeded him as pharaoh.

The history of Menetho and the Turin King List disagree as to exactly how many pharaohs ruled over the eleventh dynasty of Egypt. The Turin King List is one of many such lists created to make tracking the progression of time throughout the dynasties. As mentioned in an earlier chapter, before these king lists, dates were recorded as years of a particular pharaoh's rule (i.e. third year of Khufu, etc.) The problem with this was that as time went on, it wasn't always clear who ruled at what point in time and for how long. This was largely (though not completely) rectified through use of various king lists.

Mentuhotep's vizier was named Amenemhet (or Amenemhet.) The first pharaoh of the twelfth dynasty bore this same name. While it is possible that the ruler Amenemhet I, first king of the twelfth dynasty, used the name as a reference to the vizier, this possibility is slim, and it's generally postulated that Amenemhet I was, in fact the vizier to the last Mentuhoteps. This suggests that the previous bloodline may have been overthrown with Amenemhet I taking the throne as usurper (he ruled between 1991 and 1962 B.C.,) and some evidence may suggest a form of internal conflict during this period, however this is unconfirmed.

What is quite interesting in regard to Amenemhet is that he did not have royal blood. Although he wasn't a commoner in the sense that he worked the fields in order to sustain his living, he had no direct claim to kingship. This may also strengthen the case of usurpation. In a papyrus that Amenemhet is said to have commissioned, he claims that he was destined to be king.

This particular prophecy is notable as it was claimed to have been written at some point during the old kingdom, however, all indications show that it would have been during Amenemhet I's time. This seems to be one of the earliest (if not the earliest) uses of propaganda by a political leader.

Like the kings of the previous dynasty, he had a Horus name. This name was Weham-mswe, or "Repeater of births," or "Repetition of birth." It is postulated that Amenemhet used this name to signify a period of regrowth and further reunification of the land. Although the pharaohs of the previous dynasty were credited with reuniting Egypt, which, to a certain degree, they did, it was particularly during the twelfth dynasty that this reunification found an increase in strength and stability.

Amenemhet would move the capitol of Egypt yet again. This time from Thebes, well in the south, to a location which is somewhat vague to us today; but somewhere in the Faiyum region. This capitol was called Amenemhet-itj-tawy, or "Amenemhet, seizer/binder of the two lands." The name of this city would tell the people of Egypt that unification had happened, and was to stay that way under his rule and that of his dynasty.

The tombs of this period were much more intricate than those of the eleventh dynasty and much more elaborate than those of the first intermediate period. Amenemhet himself commissioned a pyramid of his own. It didn't have the scale or the grandeur of the pyramids of Khufu or Sneferu, however, it did utilize a traditional entrance. That is, the entrance faced the North Star. This likely symbolized that just as the North Star was unmoving in the night-sky, so would the pharaoh be constant and eternal.

Another mark of the twelfth dynasty is that the artisans, who had lost much of their skill by the time the eleventh dynasty came along, began to create much more intricate statues, sculptures and other works, the likes of which are much more familiar to us today.

Before his death, Amenemhet did something which was unusual, and possibly entirely new for the pharaohs of Egypt. Approximately ten years before his death, he made his son coregent or co-ruler of Egypt. The reason behind this seems to hearken back to the collapse of the old kingdom when Pepi, the last of the old kingdom's pharaohs, died without a viable heir to the throne.

While sources are uncertain, it appears that Amenemhet may have been assassinated. This makes the "training," if you will, of his son and heir, Senusret I particularly important. Not only was the new pharaoh of the royal bloodline, he was also very well-prepared to be king. This custom of exalting one's heir while the pharaoh was still alive and at rule would continue on even through the new kingdom.

Senusret I, who reigned from about 1971-1926 B.C., carried on the fortification of Egypt and expansion into other areas, specifically the land of Kush (later Nubia, present day Sudan.) Here he built massive fortresses to not only instill his presence, but to preserve it as well. The journey to the land of Kush was primarily to gain more resources. He also led expeditions into the Wadi Hammamat to collect materials for buildings, tombs, etc.

One of the sites that would receive the greatest amount of attention during this time was called Heliopolis (a later Greek name meaning "City of the Sun.") Heliopolis was the home of the sun cult or cult of Ra (or Re.) In the area of Heliopolis, still stands one of the obelisks from Sesostris's time. This obelisk is sixty-seven feet tall and weighs in at an impressive 120 tons. Apart from Heliopolis itself, many other architectural wonders would be created including obelisks, temples, chapels, tombs and even a pyramid for Sesostris himself.

Sesostris would follow in his father's footsteps in two ways, one, he utilized propaganda to declare himself the rightful ruler and heir of Amenemhet, his father. This papyrus is purported to be Amenemhet's advice to his son regarding how to rule the kingdom. What makes it particularly obvious that Amenemhet couldn't have written this, was that it references his own murder. While they pharaohs were considered gods, and the papyrus doesn't specifically mention the killing itself, it does give an idea of the events which possibly led to Amenemhet's demise in 1962 B.C.

The other thing that Sesostris did like his father was he had his own son made coregent of Egypt. His son was named Amenemhet II after his grandfather, the father of Sesostris and the first pharaoh of the twelfth dynasty.

Although Amenemhet II would rule for a reasonably long time (1929-1895) very little is known about him. It is known that he sent an expedition to Wadi Hammamat, constructed a white pyramid, and that the powers of Egypt were wide-reaching. In fact, even in areas of the Middle East, such as Lebanon have been excavated which have shown trade-goods bearing the name of Amenemhet II. The period of Amenemhet II's rule was marked largely by a prolific amount of international trade.

Sesostris II (ruled 1897-1878 B.C. although the length of his reign is heavily disputed) was made coregent by his father Amenemhet II, and would soon rule over the land. One thing particularly notable about Sesostris II is that he was much more focused on peace between nearby lands than many of his predecessors. During his reign, we see increased stability and inspection and rebuilding of fortresses. His power was more consolidated and he took steps to ensure its continuation through such means.

Diplomatic relations with Syria and Palestine were continued and strengthened. Along with this, he focused a great deal on the Faiyum region, a depression or oasis near the area of Cairo. He planned and carried out massive irrigation projects through the Faiyum area.

His son was Sesostris III. Sesostris III was an enormous man by the standards of ancient Egypt, and quite tall by our standards today at 6' 6". His reign saw a push to occupy more lands in Nubia, the construction of a canal to bypass the first cataract on the Nile (section of river rapids or waterfall) and, although he was a very militaristic leader, especially in the early to midpoint of his reign, these very campaigns would ensure a level of peace and prosperity.

The nomarchs during this time had grown again in and affluence, but Sesostris III's reign actually saw a shift in power from the regional nomarchs to the pharaoh in a way that belied the wealth of the nomarchs.

With Amenemhet III, a shift in tradition occurred. Like his father, statues depicting him were different from those in the past. The pharaoh was depicted as having a weary expression. One of the possible reasons for this can be found in Amenemhet's pyramid.

Amenemhet III's pyramid was constructed in a way to deter, probably originally to prevent, grave robbing. All of the pyramids previous to Amenemhet III's had entrances on the north side, pointing toward the North Star. Amenemhet III's, however, had an entrance on the south side. While it was still eventually robbed, it made location of the entrance much more difficult for archaeologists to find as it was oriented on the opposite side of what these investigators were used to. In fact, when the pyramid was first accessed, it was entered through digging and removing stones from the top.

The inside of this pyramid also offered false passageways or dead ends: likely also to deter grave robbers from reaching the king's chamber.

Another thing that Amenemhet did was continue trying to connect the waters of the Nile with the Faiyum area. He not only expanded the canal, but also constructed a dam. Work on this area which would come to be known as Lake Moeris wouldn't be finished until his son, Amenemhet IV.

Amenemhet IV built the only temple from the middle kingdom period which survives to a reasonable degree today, although even this temple in the Faiyum area is largely in ruin. Amenemhet is often referred to as the last real king of the middle kingdom.

After Amenemhet IV, the next pharaoh was a woman, likely his step-sister or aunt, though it is theorized that she may have been his wife. Her name was Sobeknefru.

Precious little is known about the rule of Sobeknefru, other than it was after her short reign that the political structure of Egypt would collapse and enter into the second intermediate period.

CHAPTER 5

Moving Toward the New Kingdom

The second intermediate period would be a time of weakening pharaotic power, it would be a time of invasion and occupation, and it would eventually see Egypt rising up again. As you look through various other great civilizations throughout the world and throughout history, very seldom do you see a civilization return from collapse, much less twice. This would be, however, exactly what happened in Egypt.

The second intermediate period and the collapse of the power structure in Egypt didn't happen overnight. What we can see though, looking at the history of this time is a continual weakening of the pharaohs' power and influence.

With the thirteenth dynasty, of which little is known about, there are still some temples, pyramids and sculptures constructed. This shows that things didn't just collapse quickly into anarchy like the first inter-mediate period is thought to have done, however, there is a distinct weakening of the power of the pharaohs and the reach of Egypt.

The middle period had lasted from 2055-1650 (or 2125-1782 depending on source) B.C., and had seen a regrowth and expansion that hadn't been conceptualized since the old kingdom. However, things start to fail.

The fourteenth dynasty moved the capitol from the Faiyum region to the area of the Nile delta to the north. This change in location shows that the fourteenth dynasty may have been more concerned with invasion from the north, from the Mediterranean Sea. It could also suggest that these rulers had no actual claim to heirship, although this is uncertain at best.

It was with the fifteenth dynasty that everything would change. The fifteenth dynasty was made up of Hyksos. Hyksos used to be translated as "shepherd kings." However, in more recent years, it has been more commonly accepted as meaning "foreign kings." It's uncertain exactly who these people were, although it's likely that they came from Palestine and/or Syria.

The other perplexing thing about the Hyksos is that we're not entirely certain whether they took power as invaders through military action, or whether they were merely immigrants and the descendants of immigrants who seized power peacefully having lived in Egypt for an elongated period of time.

We do know that the Hyksos had begun to take power during the middle kingdom in the area of the delta, a region of Egypt where immigrants and foreigners were much more commonplace. The capitol was now at Avaris in the north, and this dynasty did not have complete control of the land.

Here we see the real fissures in what had been a very productive and unified middle kingdom. In fact, it would be this disjunction of power that would result in the rise of the sixteenth dynasty.

The sixteenth dynasty of Egypt probably ruled from Thebes, although there are conflicting accounts. This dynasty did not last very long and was plagued by battles against the surviving fifteenth dynasty to the north. There were small times of peace, but the rulers of the fifteenth dynasty had many victories in the south, including the eventual conquering of the city of Thebes. This dynasty is often not considered to have actual ruling power as the fifteenth dynasty in the north continued until the rise of the seventeenth dynasty.

As if two dynasties going at the same time weren't bad enough for the already fractured Egypt, discoveries in the last twenty years or so have shown that there were also dynastic rulers in Abydos during the same time as the fifteenth and sixteenth dynasties. It is obvious that this period was a time of enormous fragmentation of power, near constant conflict between these powers and an Egypt which would not see unification for quite some time.

It's with the seventeenth dynasty that things finally start to come together for the Egyptians again. During the time just before the rise of the seventeenth dynasty, the Hyksos of the fifteenth dynasty were still at rule in the north but, apart from putting down the warring faction of the sixteenth dynasty, they generally preferred to stay up north. The city of Thebes at this time was ruled by princes, Theban princes. It was from these princes that the seventeenth dynasty would rise.

There is a papyrus which, though largely a work of fiction, gives us an idea of what happened between the Hyksos of the fifteenth dynasty and the Theban princes of the seventeenth. The story goes that the King Apophis of the Hyksos sent a missive to Sekhemre-Heruhirmaat Intef, the Theban who would become the first pharaoh of the seventeenth dynasty. These cities were somewhere around five-hundred miles apart, yet King Aphophis complained that the hippopotamuses in Sekhemre's area were keeping him from sleeping. In the fiction, Sekhemre's then leads a bunch of troops against the petulant king.

While this version is beyond unlikely, it is true that Sekhemre would lead a campaign against Pharaoh Apophis in the north. This campaign wasn't successful, however the future campaigns of his descendants would be.

These pharaohs continued their campaign against the Hyksos of Lower Egypt, having increased success in their campaigns, but it wasn't until Ahmose I that the Hyksos were finally driven out and the eighteenth dynasty, and thus the new kingdom, began.

CHAPTER 6

The New Kingdom Flourishes

With the advent of the eighteenth dynasty, the Hyk sos had been chased out of Egypt and the new king-dom (approx. 1550-1077 B.C.) was established. This wasn't enough for Ahmose, however, as he pursued the Hyksos and captured many settlements outside of Egypt along the way. He also reinforced the western border. This was to deter and protect against another Hyksos invasion, or an invasion of the Hyksos allies. During this time, a permanent army was established. This would have a great impact on the new kingdom.

When Ahmose finally returned to rule as the sole pharaoh of Egypt, Thebes was officially established as the capitol of Egypt. Egypt, during the second inter-mediate period and the fifteenth dynasty, had a cou-ple of different capitols as the country was not uni-fied as it once was: one at Thebes and one in the north. Ahmose quickly established this new capitol and began his reign by building monuments to his mother and grandmother. It would be a mark of the new kingdom that women were held in much higher regard.

Ahmose would not cease his military campaigns. After the expulsion of the Hyksos, he set his sights on Nubia. Along with having valuable resources, Nubian archers (often referred to as bowmen) were a threat that Ahmose did not want to ignore. Whether there were any indications of planned campaigns by the Nubians against the Egyptians is speculative and doubtful. What we do know is that the campaign was a success for the Egyptians.

Here it is interesting to note the way that Egyptians would count the number of men they had killed in battle. The Egyptians liked to keep track of everything of a battle (with the exception of battles they lost which were generally not mentioned.) To that end, they would bring along scribes to keep track of the spoils of victory and the amount of men slain.

The way that the scribes would count the numbers of enemy dead is that the soldiers would cut off the right hand of the slain enemy and toss them in a pile in the center of the battlefield. This way, the scribe could make an accurate (or reasonably accurate) count of the number of men slain. It wasn't uncommon for warriors to brag, boast and in some instances be rewarded for the number of hands that they took.

After a long and successful rule in which Ahmose I gave his wife a title translating to "wife of a god," the rule of Egypt would pass to his son Amenhotep I.

Amenhotep I, like his father was a warlike pharaoh. He continued to campaign against the Nubians and, according to one source, in a massive battle, he either killed or made them captives. None were said to have escaped. The scale of this is probably a reference to those who were in the battle and not the Nubians as a whole, but we do see quite a few captives taken at this time.

The army during this point in time was very well established. Training started young with some trainees beginning as young as age five. The training consisted of a number of things. In order to demoralize recruits and thus make them more suggestible to orders and training, recruits were given a intense beating. After this, they would undergo many other training programs including sword fighting, throwing knives, using sandbags to lift weights, boxing, wrestling, bow and arrow training and chariot riding. Although formal military service didn't begin until age twenty, many Egyptians began their path in the military at a very young age.

Unlike times past when Egypt didn't have a standing army, this army was well-trained, disciplined and most importantly for the recruits, they could work their way up the ranks. This was a big deal for commoners who had previously been more or less stuck in their station before the new kingdom, but it had a profound impact on the number of recruits who were willing to join and the morale of the army as a whole.

One of the more interesting things about Amenhotep I is that he was the first pharaoh in the known history of Egypt to have a separation between his mortuary temple and his tomb. This was unique in that pharaohs before him had both their tomb and their temple quite close to one another, so that their spirits would be close to the offerings of food, drinks, etc. that the priests would bring to the temple. It's likely that Amenhotep did this to discourage grave-robbing.

When Amenhotep I died, he did not have a male heir. This being the case, it was Thutmose I, a commoner who married the daughter of King and Queen Ahmose Nefertari. It was due to this marriage that he was able to take the throne. Because Amenhotep didn't have a son, the succession was based off of who would marry and bear children of the "purest" royal blood. Incest was common among the pharaohs and their queens during Ancient Egypt, much like it would be for millennia afterward in other monarchist societies. The reason for this was the preservation of the royal blood. Although Thutmose did not himself have royal blood, due to his marriage with the daughter of Ahmose, he was close enough.

Like his predecessors he entered Nubia in order to gain resources and exert his power, however, he went much farther down the Nile than those who came before him. One of the men who joined his was named Ahmose, son of Ebana (not to be confused with pharaoh Ahmose.) Ahmose, son of Ebana had campaigned with two previous pharaohs by this time, Ahmose I (1549-1524) and Amenhotep I (1524-1503.)

By this point in his life, Ahmose, son of Ebana would have been well into his fifties, and the journey was perilous. Regardless, with Ahmose, son of Ebana at his side, Thutmose I would conquer two of the Nubian tribes and also a group of Bedouins (people of the desert.) As if that wasn't a large enough display of power, he also erected an enormous stelé, claiming the fifth cataract (up until then, well into Nubian territory) as the southern border of the land of Egypt. And, just for good measure, he pinned the body of a Nubian leader upside down and dead from the prow of his ship. The body would remain there until he returned to Thebes.

Thutmose I was far from finished though. He and his army would continue on and march far north to Mesopotamia, conquering as they went. When he reached his destination, he erected a large stelé here as well, claiming this as the northern border of Egypt.

At his death, Thutmose would be the first pharaoh to be buried in the Valley of the Kings on the west bank of the Nile near Thebes. This would come to be a trend among future pharaohs. The Valley of the Kings became popular as a burial site due to several factors that it was so arid and barren (it still is to this day) that neither Thutmose I or those who would follow him would have to worry about settlements cropping up around the site. Another reason is that the top of the mountain in the area is a natural pyramid-like point. This would have been appealing as a reference to the incredible monuments of the past. Last, but not least, is the fact that there is only one way in or out of this area. That would have been much easier to guard. Although this didn't entirely deter grave-robbers, it went a long way to preserving many of the artifacts that we have today.

Upon Thutmose's death, though he had fathered three sons and two daughters, all but one daughter had died. Her name was Hatshepsut. She would have been only twelve years (or so) at the time of her father's death, but with no other heirs with pure royal blood, it came to one of Thutmose's sons from a con-current marriage, also named Thutmose, to marry Hatshepsut and become pharaoh.

In Egypt, it was common for the pharaoh to have multiple wives, but there was a structure to this. The pharaoh would have one "great wife," this would be the woman from whom the first heirs would be chosen. These were the heirs thought to be of purest blood. The pharaoh also had other wives. These wives were still highly regarded within the house, but there was only ever one great wife. If there was no viable heir from the union with the great wife, the heir would then be chosen from among the children of these wives. There were also consorts of the pharaoh. These wives were by no means disrespected, in fact, they were highly revered. It was from the consorts that the pharaoh's heir would come should no viable heir be chosen from the great wife's children (if she had any) or the wives' children (if they had any.) Thutmose II would have been the son of one of Thutmose I's wives, Mutnofret.

Thutmose II was married to Hatshepsut for twenty years until his death. When he died, the question came again, "Who is going to be pharaoh?" Thutmose II had a son by another woman. He was Thutmose III. He would have been Hatshepsut's step-son and, due to the fact that Thutmose II was her half-brother, Thutmose III would have also been her nephew. He would become one of the most remarkable pharaohs of all Egypt's history.

Before Thutmose III could take power though, he had to grow up. He would have been about six or seven years old at this time. Therefore, Hatshepsut became regent. That is, acting pharaoh until Thutmose III grew to the proper age. At one point, however, Hatshepsut would declare herself king. She would be

Martin R. Phillips

pharaoh and even went so far as to don the "false beard of authority" which the pharaohs are often seen wearing in their kas or other depictions.

Hatshepsut's reign would be a remarkable one. She would build an incredible monument which still stands today. It would depict numerous things, but largely it would depict an expedition into the land of Punt (location still unknown,) that she sent. The drawings inside Hatshepsut's monument would be the first accurate depiction of the area that was visited. Hatshepsut also instituted the first zoo in the history of the world. The expedition to Punt would return with many treasures including animals, incense and, notably, trees from which the incense was made. These were brought back to Thebes and planted.

She would also erect four obelisks on the east bank of Thebes at Karnack temple. One of the most interesting things that Hatshepsut had included inside her monument was that of her divine birth. This was by no means a new custom. Most pharaohs, at least of the time, would depict their "divine birth" in the very same way (that of being molded on a potter's wheel) by the god Khnum, the god who created all humans according the ancient Egyptians. Whether it was a mistake of those who did the inscriptions, or something that Hatshepsut decided herself, she was depicted (with her ka, as was always present in such hieroglyphs) as being formed a male. Although many of the aspects of Hatshepsut's reign could be misconstrued that she was attempting to masquerade as a man, this was not the case. She was a proud woman, and referred to herself as "the female/woman falcon."

Also, according to the walls of the monument, the god Amun came to Hatshepsut's mother, Ahmose, in her husband's form. Ahmose then lied with the god and became pregnant with Hatshepsut. This was the mythos created to signify her right to rule as pharaoh.

Hatshepsut also erected two tombs for herself. One was built as the tomb of the Queen of Egypt, which she had been for some time, however, the one which she favored and to which she committed her earthly remains was in the Valley of the Kings.

Though Thutmose III would grow to adulthood during Hatshepsut's continued reign, she remained pharaoh for the remainder of her life. When Thutmose III finally became pharaoh, a little more of the story comes out in what he does regarding the places in which Hatshepsut's name is carved. He removes her name entirely. After removing her name, he adds in the names of his forefathers, Thutmose I, Thutmose II and, in some cases, his own name. Where this begins to grow a bit clearer is that in a couple of places, Hatshepsut is depicted, standing in front of Thutmose III. He had grown to adulthood a while before the end of Hatshepsut's reign, however, it seems that she may have used her influence as pharaoh to keep him from taking power until her death. This seems to be the reason behind Thutmose attempting to erase her name from history; however, evidence shows that this may not actually have been done out of spite. It is more than likely that the Egyptians of the time simply wanted to remove record of a woman being pharaoh. Regardless of how it happened, Hatshepsut was one of the most influential pharaohs of all ancient Egypt.

Thutmose III is most widely regarded as the most successful warlike pharaoh of ancient Egypt. He would send forth many campaigns to various parts of the nearby world. It's likely that while Hatshepsut was ruling, he was in the military being trained, learning strategy and developing the skills that would make him such a successful warlord.

His first campaign was to Megiddo. While Hatshepsut was pharaoh, she led few military campaigns, and the Syrro-Palestine (area of modern-day Syria and Palestine) people had stopped paying their tribute to Egypt for the most part. This was tolerated under Hatshepsut's rule, but as the Syrro-Palestinians began to grow more independent, Thutmose III decided that something would have to be done.

He led his army through a narrow valley, surprising the army of Megiddo well outside the city walls and utterly dominating them in combat. The army of

Megiddo retreated into the city and was able to regroup. Because the Egyptians were busier plundering the fallen enemies than they were with finishing the job against their living enemies, they had to lay siege to the city of Megiddo for a period of seven months. After the long siege, the walls of Megiddo finally fell and Thutmose III took the city.

The next eighteen years would see return trips to Syrro-Palestine to "remind" the Syrians of their duty to send tribute to Egypt. He would also campaign to Phoenician coastal outposts which were changed into Egyptian bases. He would also take Kadesh and other cities in and around the Bekaa region and also Mitanni. Thutmose III would die in 1425 B.C.

Thutmose III's successor was Amenhotep II. He would preserve the expanded kingdom that his father had built, however, during his reign came a sort of peace between Egypt and Syrro-Palestine.

Amenhotep II's successor was Thutmose IV. Thutmose IV wasn't intended to be the heir to the throne, however it is likely that he usurped power by stepping in front of his brother. He would commission what is called "The Dream Stelé," a move that would attempt to justify why he, and not his older brother would take the throne. Thutmose IV is most well-known for restoring the Sphinx.

Under Thutmose IV's son, Amenhotep III, pharaoh after his father's death in 1391 B.C., Egypt would see an age of prosperity and artistic accomplishment. Of all of the pharaohs throughout the history of ancient Egypt, more statues of Amenhotep III survive today than any other. It was in his son, however, that many historians are more interested.

Amenhotep III's son was named Amenhotep IV. Many people aren't familiar with the name Amenhotep IV. That's because only a few years into his reign, he changed his name to Akhenaten.

Akhenaten (reigned 1351–1334 B.C.) is known best for turning his back on the religion of Egypt in a big way. The Egyptians had been polytheistic (belief in more than one god) for as long as history has records, however, Akenaten instituted worship of the sun-disk, called Aten. In fact, the name Akhenaten means "Effective/Effectual for Aten." The thing is, only he and his family were actually allowed to worship Aten. The rest of Egypt was meant to worship him. This makes his change not to monotheism, rather to a ditheistic religion. Akhenaten is also well known because of his wife, Nefertiti.

Nefertiti is somewhat an enigma as it seems that nobody knows where she came from. There are theories as to her heritage, but these are unconfirmed. Just as mysteriously as she came into the picture, so would she fade back out of it. However, she has been immortalized in the now iconic bust that was made of her.

This period of the new kingdom would come to be known as the Amarna period, due to the advent of Akhenaten's city of the same name. Although this was a primary goal, from what we know, of his leadership, this change would not last.

There is some dispute as to who came next. The records of this period are largely destroyed by the future kings who would reinstitute the full pantheon of Egyptian gods.

Both of Akhenaten's possible successors also subscribed to the Amarna principle. One of them was named Smenkhkare. Not much is known of Smenkhkare, largely due to the fact that future pharaohs would seek to destroy evidence of the Armana period as referenced above.

The other possible successor was named Neferneferuaten. It's debated whether Neferneferuaten was a man or a woman, or was actually Nefertiti or Smenkhkare. What is known is who came next.

King Tut, as he's commonly referred to in colloquial conversation today was the young Pharaoh Tutankhamen. Tutankhamen was the son of Akhenaten. The way that we know this with such certainty is that the DNA of both Akhenaten and Tut were tested against each other and Tutankhamen was found to be the son.

Pharaoh Tutankhamen is, quite honestly, best known due to the fact that his tomb was relatively intact when it was discovered. His burial mask has become iconic for ancient Egypt, although Tut would not have been pharaoh for very long, likely nine years. This rule would have been from the age of nine to the age of eighteen, the time of his death (1323 B.C.)

Rumors persisted for quite a while, and sometimes to this day, about the "curse of King Tut's tomb," however this was simply an invention created to sell newspapers after the discovery of the child-pharaoh's burial chamber. Those who unearthed the chamber and remains of Tutankhamen did not die statistically sooner than others of the time-period.

Exactly how Tutankhamen died is still debated to this day. The evidence is that he had a broken leg near the time of his death which became infected. He also carried malaria. He could possibly have suffered from epilepsy. Regardless how he died, the poor kid had a lot going wrong.

The pharaoh who succeeded Tutankhamen was Ay. Ay would only rule for four years, and he would be the last of the Amarna pharaohs. It is possible that Ay was regent during the time of Tut, although this is uncertain.

With Horemheb, the eighteenth dynasty would come to a close. He would work to undo the Amarna philosophy/religion that had been instituted by his predecessors. He destroyed many monuments of the previous pharaohs, and would often reuse them for his own means. He was likely childless at his death. This brought the eighteenth dynasty to its end.

CHAPTER 7

The New Kingdom Continue and Ends

It is with the continuation and end of the new king-dom that this book will end. Although ancient Egypt would go through a third intermediate period, a brief attempt at revival and eventually come under the rule of the Greeks and later, the Romans, the fall of the new kingdom was in many ways the end of the road for the grandiose history of Ancient Egypt.

The first pharaoh of the nineteenth dynasty was Ramses I. He ruled for a very brief period, and not much is known of his reign, other than that it was a time of transition from the eighteenth dynasty to the nineteenth.

Ramses I's son, however, would undertake campaigns to attempt to restore the grandeur which was seen in the eighteenth dynasty. He would attack the Hittites and the Libyans, and would even take the great city of Kadesh, however, he would return the rule of this city to Hatti in an attempt to make peace.

Ramses II (also known as Ramses the Great and often known for his role in the story of Moses) would attempt to retake Kadesh. Ramses II had a very long rule as pharaoh (approx. 1279-1213 B.C.) During this time, he would battle against pirates, campaign in Syria many times and send armies against the Nubians and the Libyans.

During the early years of his reign, however, Ramses II was much more concerned with building. He would build monuments, temples and even cities such as Pi-Ramesses where he would establish a new capitol in Egypt. This city was located in a very meaningful place. It was built on the ruins of Avaris, the city from which the Hyksos had reigned.

Under the rule of Ramses II, Egypt had an enormous influx of wealth due to his many military campaigns and tributes paid him by the peoples which he conquered. Ramses is thought to have died at around the age of ninety having become quite unhealthy due to severe arthritis and dental problems.

One interesting fact about Ramses is that his hair was blonde, but he likely dyed it red using henna, an herb.

After the incredibly prosperous rule of Ramses II came Merneptah. The thirteenth son of Ramses II, he was the oldest surviving child of his father at the time of the old pharaoh's death. He would have been late in life himself, particularly for the time-period, aged somewhere between sixty and seventy years old. He would send military campaigns like his father, although not nearly to such a great extent. It is with the successors (note the plural) of Merneptah that things would really start taking a nose-dive in the great land.

Seti II was the rightful heir to succeed Merneptah, however, his reign was challenged by Amenmesse from Thebes. Amenmesse would take a great portion of Upper Egypt, including the kingdom of Kush. Although Seti II was able to retake the lands which Amenmesse had claimed, the infighting was becoming great within the nineteenth dynasty.

Siptah, the son of either Seti II or Amenmesse, would be the second to last ruler in the nineteenth dynasty. Like Tutankhamen, he would die at a very young age and may or may not have actually held complete control of the station of pharaoh, as his stepmother Twosret was regent due to his youth. She would rule after his death for a period of only two years or so. With her death, the nineteenth dynasty would end.

Setnakhte was the first pharaoh of the twentieth dynasty, and would only enjoy a very short reign. It's not entirely clear how he came to power, as he was of no blood relation to Siptah or Twosret. It's possible that he usurped the throne. During his short time as pharaoh, he did, however, manage to largely stabilize Egypt, although this would not last long.

The son of Setnakhte was Ramses III. Often considered to be the last pharaoh of the new kingdom with any remarkable power or control over the land, the reign of Ramses III would see near-constant battle and invasion. Due to the constant warfare, the wealth of Egypt would not-so-slowly diminish and leave a weakened nation for his son to inherit.

Ramses IV was what we would now consider middle-aged by the time he took the throne. His father had ruled for approximately thirty years. He would begin many building projects, but his reign was cut short as he died after only five or six years as pharaoh.

Ramses V's (if you're starting to notice a pattern of names, you're on the right track) reign would be marked by the growing influence of the cult of Amun, and the continued decrease of the wealth of the pharaoh and Egypt (often due to the demands of the priests themselves.)

The rules of Ramses VI, VII and VIII were similar in a few ways: First, they all ruled for short periods of time (Ramses VI for about eight years, Ramses VII for about seven years and Ramses VIII for about one year.) Also, the state of Egypt was declining faster and faster at this point. Even with the building projects of Ramses IX who enjoyed a much longer reign (about eighteen years,) the pharaohs were on a steady downward decline, and it didn't seem like there was much to be done about it.

The last two pharaohs of the twentieth dynasty (final of the new kingdom) were Ramses X and Ramses XI respectively. It is my opinion, although unconfirmed that these rulers had stuck with the name Ramses so long as an attempt to recapture the glory of Ramses the Great (Ramses II.)

Not much is known of Ramses X's short rule, and the exact period of his reign is still largely disputed for this fact. With Ramses XI, however, an increase in longevity would not postpone the fall of the once-great new kingdom of Egypt. Ramses XI would rule for a length of 29-33 years.

Civil unrest, increasing times of drought and famine and the loss of Egypt's wealth would lead to the end of the twentieth dynasty and the new kingdom. This would lead to the third intermediate period.

CONCLUSION

Thanks again for reading this book!

The end of the new kingdom marks, in many ways, the end of Egypt as it once had been. The great pharaohs and times of prosperity had passed and Egypt would slip into a third intermediate period, including subjugation by the Persian Empire.

Though the new pharaohs would temporarily throw off the fetters of their Persian overlords, the late period, as it was called, would be short and control of Egypt would eventually fall back to the Persians.

Egypt, once grand and autonomous, would see many other conquerors after this time, including Alexander the Great (who was named pharaoh without a fight, due to his decimation of the Persian forces and, well, basically everyone else he ran across.) The Greeks would continue to rule Egypt, being followed by Romans and Byzantines.

I hope that you have enjoyed this journey through ancient Egypt and its history. We've come through unification to great pyramids, from collapse to rebirth (a couple of times,) and finally to the new kingdom and the great pharaohs of the eighteenth and nineteenth dynasties.

The history of Egypt is long and complicated. There is much that is left unknown, dates are almost always disputed and there's no way of knowing (at least at this time) how many pharaohs and great achievements are missing from the histories. That makes what we do know about Egypt all the more special.

Ancient Egypt lasted longer than most civilizations have even existed, and modern Egypt lives today. Though many things changed during, and many more have changed since, the old, middle and new kingdoms, ancient Egypt still fascinates and inspires us with one of the most intricate and complicated histories of any civilization that has ever existed.

Though there is much that we still don't know about this powerful, often enigmatic place and time, new expeditions are still going to try to uncover the breath of the past. As technology grows more powerful, it's likely that what we know of ancient Egypt will continue to grow throughout the coming years, decades and centuries.

I hope that you have enjoyed this look at ancient Egypt as much as I have enjoyed studying and writing it.

The mark of history is a flame passed from one society to all others. One can only wonder what will be written about our society in the times to come.

Thank you,

Martin R. Phillips

A Preview of
Martin R. Phillips'
Latest Book

ANCIENT GREECE

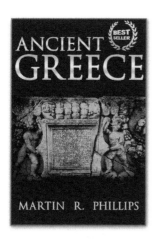

Ancient Greece is, without a doubt, one of the most fascinating cultures that our world has ever seen! Whether you look at their mythology, their history, or their philosophy, the Ancient Greek civilization has permeated our approach to, and understanding of, the world at large. It is impossible to tell the story of modern civilization without providing some recognition to the influence of Greece.

The Greek Empire was vast, encompassing over 700 individual city-states, 150-173 of which would form the Delian League in an effort to combat the onslaught of Persia. How did so many city-states come together under one rule? With only a fraction joining the Delian League, how did these city-states *stay* together in times of disagreement and conflict?

There are hundreds, if not thousands of questions regarding this vast and fascinating civilization. One could spend years and write many volumes on each period of the Ancient Grecian culture, history, and mythology. It has been my pleasure to assemble this research, and the voice of Greece itself (through reference to its own historians, including Herodotus, Thucydides, and Xenophon.) I am excited to share with you an admittedly brief look at the civilization we know as Ancient Greece (a full history would take more pages than the unabridged Oxford English Dictionary and the Encyclopedia Britannica combined.)

In this book you will find the history and opinions of the Ancient Greeks. You will discover their truth and their mythology. You will learn of war and peacetime. There are heroes and villains, saints and scoundrels. You will find philosophies that changed the world, and continue to do so even to this day.

For the most part, the contents of this book are arranged topically as opposed to strictly chronologically to allow specific areas of interest in the Ancient Greeks and their civilization to be more easily accessible. However, care has been taken to include the approximate dates of people and events to give you a good idea of the chronology of the content.

The importance of the Greek civilization cannot be overstated. In nearly every facet of our lives, we can find something which had its roots, or took a new turn in Ancient Greece. When you go to the polls to elect an official, you are operating on a Greek principle. When you discuss the nature of life with others, you are performing a modified version of the Greek symposium. Even when you sit down to watch television, or read a book, you often find references to Trojan wars, Sparta and their role in the conflict with the Persians, the philosophy, or the character of the Greeks.

As you rediscover Ancient Greece, I encourage you to make note of how much of that vast and diverse civilization still lives on throughout our world today...

PS. If you enjoyed this book, please help me out by kindly leaving a review!

48341619R00050

Made in the USA
San Bernardino, CA
23 April 2017